# The resourcing puzz

Rosalind Levačić

First published in 2005 by the Institute of Education, University of London
20 Bedford Way, London WC1H 0AL
www.ioe.ac.uk/publications

Over 100 years of excellence in education

**British Library Cataloguing in Publication Data:**
A catalogue record for this publication is available from the British Library

ISBN 0 85473 702 2

Rosalind Levačić asserts the moral right to be identified as the author of this work.

Design by Andrew Chapman
Typeset and printed by the Alden Group Ltd, Oxford, UK

# The resourcing puzzle
# The difficulties of establishing causal links between resourcing and student outcomes

Rosalind Levačić

Professor of Economics and Finance of Education

Based on a Professorial Lecture delivered at the Institute of Education, University of London on 15 June 2004

# Acknowledgements

I would like to thank John Gray and Anna Vignoles for their comments on the written version of the lecture which helped me to improve it. The remaining inadequacies are my responsibility.

Professor Rosalind Levačić

# The resourcing puzzle

## Why the resourcing puzzle?

The reason I have called this lecture the resourcing puzzle is because of the long-standing disjunction between the beliefs of parents, students and educationists that additional resources devoted to education improve students' learning outcomes and the continuing controversy amongst researchers, particularly educational economists, as to whether resources matter. The two groups rely on different sources of knowledge: the former on common sense, plausibility, personal experience, hearsay and, on occasions, self interest; the latter on variants of the scientific method applied to social settings, which may be influenced by prior political beliefs.

Compared to 20 or more years ago education is seen as far more important for contributing to improved economic performance and reduced social inequality. As more public and private resources are devoted to education so it becomes increasingly important to understand the relationships between the amounts and types of resources invested in education and the resulting outcomes for individual learners and for society. Improving the quality of education and consequently students' attainment has been a persistent theme of

UK government policy for at least two decades. As one prime minister declaimed:

> Our most important task in this Parliament is to raise the quality of education. It's in the national interest. And it's in the individual interest of every parent and above all of every child.
>
> (Margaret Thatcher: Conservative Party annual conference 1987)[1]

The current government has accorded unprecedented importance to education as the route to greater personal welfare, reducing social exclusion and improving international competitiveness and has backed its policies with substantial increases in spending (DfES 2002). Table 1 shows two measures of recurrent expenditure per pupil in real terms and the annual rate of change in these measures. Also shown is revenue funding per pupil provided by central government in the form of its own spending and the amount it calculates that local authorities need to be funded for maintaining schools (Education Formula Spending[2]). In the early 1990s, primary school expenditure grew at a modest rate while secondary expenditure fluctuated. In the mid-1990s expenditure per pupil declined. Since 1998/9 it has been rising quite rapidly at annual rates of between 5 and 9 per cent in real terms. Revenue funding per pupil indicates that the government plans to increase funding for education by over 3 per cent in real terms in the years 2003/4 and 2004/5 and by 5 per cent in 2005/6 (DfES 2004).

The rise in funding per pupil has not only increased resourcing across the board but has also been targeted at specific interventions, such as the Literacy and Numeracy strategies, Excellence in Cities, City Academies, reduction in class sizes at Key Stage 1, expansion in the number of teaching assistants and investments in ICT. All this is predicated on the belief that increased resources will improve student attainment (DfES 2002).

However, research on the relationship between resources available to schools and students' academic attainment has not provided unequivocal support for these beliefs. There is considerable controversy about whether or not the evidence produced by researchers indicates that increased resources have a positive marginal impact on student attainment. These doubts are reflected in

**Table 1** Recurrent expenditure and revenue funding per pupil 1988/98 to 2005/6 in real terms (2002/03 prices)

| | School based expenditure per pupil[a] | | | | Current education expenditure by central and local government per pupil[b] | | | | Revenue funding per pupil[c] | |
| | Nursery & primary | | Secondary | | Nursery & primary | | Secondary | | All phases of schooling | |
| | £ per pupil[d] | % annual change | £ per pupil[d] | % annual change | £ per pupil[d] | % annual change | £ per pupil[d] | % annual change | £ per pupil[d] | % annual change |
|---|---|---|---|---|---|---|---|---|---|---|
| 1988–89 | 1806 | NA | 2831 | NA | | | | | | |
| 1989–90 | 1854 | 2.7 | 2903 | 2.5 | | | | | | |
| 1990–91 | 1892 | 2.0 | 2859 | −1.5 | | | | | | |
| 1991–92 | 1956 | 3.4 | 2859 | 0.0 | | | | | | |
| 1992–93 | 2042 | 4.4 | 2913 | 1.9 | | | | | | |
| 1993–94 | 2050 | 0.4 | 2830 | −2.8 | 2065 | NA | 3001 | NA | | |
| 1994–95 | 2060 | 0.5 | 2820 | −0.4 | 2106 | 2.0 | 2996 | −0.2 | | |
| 1995–96 | 2040 | −1.0 | 2760 | −2.1 | 2156 | 2.4 | 3071 | 2.5 | 2865 | |
| 1996–97 | 2030 | −0.5 | 2740 | −0.7 | 2155 | −0.1 | 3046 | −0.8 | 2875 | 0.4 |
| 1997–98 | 1980 | −2.5 | 2680 | −2.2 | 2173 | 0.9 | 2994 | −1.7 | 2875 | 0.0 |
| 1998–99 | 2080 | 5.1 | 2700 | 0.7 | 2191 | 0.8 | 2998 | 0.2 | 2900 | 0.9 |
| 1999–00 | 2190 | 5.3 | 2790 | 3.3 | 2320 | 5.8 | 3070 | 2.4 | 3020 | 4.1 |
| 2000–01 | 2400 | 9.6 | 2990 | 7.2 | 2550 | 10.0 | 3253 | 6.0 | 3240 | 7.3 |
| 2001–02 | 2620 | 9.2 | 3210 | 7.4 | 2846 | 11.6 | 3531 | 8.6 | 3380 | 4.3 |
| 2002–03 | | | | | 2984 | 4.9 | 3599 | 1.9 | 3500 | 3.6 |
| 2003–04[e] | | | | | 3260 | 9.2 | 3782 | 5.1 | 3620 | 3.4 |

*Continued*

**Table 1** Continued

| | School based expenditure per pupil[a] | | | | Current education expenditure by central and local government per pupil[b] | | | | Revenue funding per pupil[c] | |
| | Nursery & primary | | Secondary | | Nursery & primary | | Secondary | | All phases of schooling | |
| | £ per pupil[d] | % annual change | £ per pupil[d] | % annual change | £ per pupil[d] | % annual change | £ per pupil[d] | % annual change | £ per pupil[d] | % annual change |
|---|---|---|---|---|---|---|---|---|---|---|
| 2004–05[e] | | | | | | | | | 3740 | 3.3 |
| 2005–06[e] | | | | | | | | | 3930 | 5.1 |

*Notes:*

[a] School based expenditure per pupil includes school staff costs, premises, equipment, supplies, and unspent balances: excludes special schools, LEA central administration, home to school transport and capital. Source: Statistics of Education: Education and Training Expenditure since 1993–94 (SO 2003) and since 1990–01 (SO 2000).

[b] Current expenditure on schools for under 5s, primary and secondary excluding local authority expenditure on meals, transport, non-maintained school fees, teacher development, pupil support and other support services divided by the number of pupils. Source: DFES Departmental Reports for 1999, 2001 & 2004.

[c] Revenue funding per pupil consists of Education Standard Spending Assessment/Education Formula Spending plus all school related revenue grants in DFES departmental expenditure limit for pupils aged 3–19, excluding Sure Start and Child Care. Source: DFES Departmental Reports for 1999, 2001 & 2004.

[d] All amounts are in real terms in 2002/3 prices using the GDP deflator (source: HM Treasury website).

[e] Revenue funding for years 2003–04 to 2005–06 is the planned amount.

the title of a Brookings Institution collection of papers on the effects of school resources on student achievement and adult success – *Does Money Matter?* (Burtless 1996).

In the rest of the lecture I wish to do the following:

1. give a brief review of the controversy over the evidence about whether resources matter;
2. ask why has this controversy arisen and seek the answer in the methodological problems of establishing causal relationships between social phenomena;
3. set out criteria for good quality studies of the education production function;
4. review briefly the evidence from better quality studies using UK data;
5. consider some evidence from developing countries where resourcing levels are so much lower and have greater variation;
6. report findings from an Institute of Education study which has used the better quality English data now available to estimate the relationship between school resources and attainment at Key Stage 3.

## A brief history of education production function research

The relationship between the resources used to provide education and the resulting outcomes for students is treated as analogous to a general production function in economics, in which inputs (factors of production) are related to outputs. Hence, this research is referred to as 'education production function' (EPF) research. Here I am going to restrict it to schools. The education production function is a simplification of a more complex reality. School outputs are in practice multiple and jointly produced. The education production function can only deal with one input at a time (unless they are combined in some assumed way).[3] Three main types of output or outcome are: [4]

- cognitive attainment – examination results, test scores or qualifications;

- affective outcomes (attitudes and behaviours) or non-monetary benefits in later life (e.g. better health, less criminality, lower fertility in developing countries, better parenting);
- future earnings.

Outputs may be solely private benefits to the individual concerned or they may have external or spillover benefits for others in society. Inputs may be defined as overall expenditure per pupil or as physical inputs: teacher–pupil ratio, class size, teacher characteristics/quality, non-teaching staff, materials, equipment and books, facilities/ buildings. The most usual outcomes in studies are attainment measures and earnings. Class size, pupil–teacher ratios and expenditure are the most common inputs included.

The education production function focuses on the relationship between resource inputs and student outcomes and largely ignores the complexity of the family and school processes that intervene. At a minimum, student inputs, such as ability, prior attainment, family income, education and SES, are included as these are important determinants of student outcomes. An education production function that would account for the school processes of teaching and learning would be a version of the 'context-input-process-outcome-model' which forms the theoretical basis of school effectiveness research (Teddlie and Reynolds 1999; Scheerens 1997, 1999). Student outcomes at the individual level are determined by the interaction of school context, student inputs (in particular prior attainment or ability and home background) resource inputs and school and class-level processes. The postulated causal links are from the context and input variables to school processes, which in turn determine student outcomes. Processes act at school, class/teacher and individual pupil level. While school effectiveness research focuses on the identification and explanation of differences in school and teacher effectiveness, with little interest in resources beyond class size, education production function research has concentrated on the relationship between inputs and outputs, largely treating school and classroom processes as a black box.

Education production function and school effectiveness research have a common reference point in the Coleman Report (Coleman *et al.* 1966) into educational inequality in the USA, which is usually cited as the first major study of the EPF. It found family background factors and the characteristics of the school peer group to be the major determinants of a child's attainment and that the school attended and the amount spent on schools had little effect by comparison. School effectiveness research from the late 1970s onwards produced evidence of differential school effects. Economists developed a separate line of research investigating the relationship between school inputs and student attainment, but with little examination of processes within schools. Mostly this research has been conducted in the USA. One economist in particular, Hanushek (1979, 1986, 1997, 1998) has clocked up numerous citations through publishing several literature reviews of these studies. His summary conclusion from reviewing some 90 studies with 377 estimates is that:

> there is no strong or consistent relationship between school resources and student performance. In other words there is little reason to be confident that simply adding more resources to schools as currently constituted will yield performance gains among students. . . . Substantial evidence suggests that there are large differences among teachers and schools but these are not related to teacher salaries or to measured resources.
>
> (Hanushek 1997: 148)

From these findings Hanushek and others have drawn important policy conclusions. They explain the absence of a consistent relationship between school inputs and student outcomes by schools' being inefficient and argue that there is no point spending more on schools until the school system is redesigned to give schools incentives to be efficient. These incentives are provided by parental choice, greater competition between schools, pupil-led funding, performance-related pay, clear attainment targets for state schools and information to parents about schools' success in meeting them.

Hanushek's conclusions have not gone unchallenged. In particular his choice of studies and method of counting findings have been criticised. He counted as a separate 'study' each regression for a different outcome measure in the same publication and did not select studies for his reviews using explicit criteria for high quality studies. Hedges *et al.* (1994), from a meta-analysis of US studies meeting explicit quality criteria, concluded that for per-pupil expenditure, teacher ability, experience and salary, and class size there was evidence of positive effects on student outcomes and no evidence of negative effects. Contrary to Hanushek, they concluded that 'school resources are systematically related to student achievement and these relations are large enough to be educationally important'. But they agreed that efficiency incentives are important for how educators use resources. Dewey *et al.* (2000) reworked Hanushek's data and found stronger evidence for significant positive effects and weaker evidence for significant negative effects. Krueger (2003) demonstrates how Hanushek (1997) biased his conclusions for class size by the relative weights he chose to give the studies. If studies are equally weighted (rather than the number of reported regressions per study) and if in addition studies are weighted by quality as judged by publication source, the proportion of significant positive findings increases and that of negative significant findings decreases, as shown in Table 2. Even so, the evidence in favour of positive class size effects in Table 2 is not overwhelming. Krueger examined in detail nine studies to which Hanushek gave particular weight (127 estimates extracted out of 277 on class size) and finds that most were not designed to address class size per se but focused on the relationship between other variables and student attainment. Reviewing US research on the effect of school inputs on earnings Card and Kreuger (1996) concluded that a 10 per cent increase in school spending is associated with a 1–2 per cent increase in annual earnings in later life – a conclusion challenged by Betts (1996) in the same volume.

This on-going controversy illustrates how the problems of interpreting research findings are exacerbated when many of the published studies are poor, usually due to lack of appropriate data and mis-specified models.

## Methodological issues

The crucial issue in this field of research, as in others in the social sciences concerned ultimately with improving policy responses to social issues through

**Table 2** The effects of giving different weightings to education production function studies for the summary conclusions about the direction of the findings

| Result with respect to effect of class size on student attainment | Hanushek's findings (weighted by number of regression results) % | Studies equally weighted % | Studies weighted by journal impact[1] % |
|---|---|---|---|
| Positive significant | 14.8 | 25.5 | 34.5 |
| Positive Insignificant | 26.7 | 27.1 | 21.2 |
| Negative significant | 13.4 | 10.3 | 6.9 |
| Negative insignificant | 25.3 | 23.1 | 25.4 |
| Unknown | 19.9 | 14.0 | 12.0 |

*Source:* Krueger (2003).
*Note:*
[1] The journal impact weighting is taken from the Institute for Scientific Information and weights journals according to the average number of citations to the journal in 1998.

better evidence of policy impacts, is uncovering and measuring causal relationships. This knowledge is crucial for finding policy instruments that government can manipulate in order to achieve desired policy effects. By causation we generally mean that if one variable, X, is changed then that results in a change, which may be positive or negative, in another variable, Y, and that the direction of the change is from X to Y. For example, a reduction in class size results in an increase in pupil attainment.

$$X \implies Y$$

A causal relationship need not be deterministic. It is sufficient if X (the cause) increases the probability of Y (the effect) happening. It is well known that if two variables are observed to be correlated this does not imply causation, since they may be both caused by a third unobserved variable. Hence it is necessary to define causality in counterfactual terms (Sobel 1998).[5] An event X causes an effect Y if Y occurs in the presence of X but, other things remaining the same, does not occur if X is not present. The counterfactual here is not X.

However, a causal relation as the one above is not a causal process – that is it does not explain how the relationship comes about (Salmon 1998). We can observe that reducing class size, keeping other factors unchanged, causes an increase in pupil achievement but not understand the causal mechanisms that bring about the causal effect. It is, of course, desirable to understand the causal mechanisms that produce a causal effect. The main point here is that the causal effect and the causal mechanism are two distinct aspects of causality. In many situations where patterns of social behaviour are being investigated, quantitative data are required for the identification of causal impacts but these data often give limited insights into causal mechanisms. Qualitative evidence is valuable in providing explanations of causal mechanisms, especially when linked to quantitative evidence of impact (Tashakkori and Teddlie 2003).

If we wish to discover whether being taught in a smaller class has a causal effect on a child's attainment then we need to observe the effects on the same child of being taught in a larger and in a smaller class with all other conditions remaining the same. This is naturally impossible. The next best alternative is randomly to assign a large number of children to large and small classes and observe differences in their attainment over time. Random assignment with a large enough sample ensures that the control and treatment groups contain the same distribution of all other factors that affect attainment, other than class size, so that any difference in average attainment between the two groups can be attributed to the difference in class size. Any difference between the attainment of the treated group (in small classes) and those in the control group (large classes) is the estimated average treatment effect. This does of course assume that the random controlled trial (RCT) has been well conducted. The main point for the present is that the RCT is the closest research design to creating the counterfactual. As far as education production function research is concerned, the Tennessee STAR experiment with small class size for kindergarten children is the best known attempt at implementing an RCT (Finn and Achilles 1999; Krueger and Whitmore 2001; Nye *et al.* 2002; Ritter and Boruch 1999). Most STAR studies, though not all, have found that smaller classes raised achievement, in particular for socially disadvantaged children.

There are well-known difficulties with designing and implementing well executed random control trials. In education there are often ethical and political objections to favouring some students with increased resources. These objections seem to have far less weight in medical research, which relies on the RCT. Further problems with RCTs are that the value of the random assignment for preventing bias can be undermined by attrition, by the treated not taking up the treatment and by people in the control group securing treatment. Treatment and control groups are aware of which they are, as an educational placebo is very difficult to devise, and this can affect behaviour and bias results. It may well be difficult to replicate experimental results in education to the general population because of differences between the experimental treatment group and the general population or because of behavioural responses to the policy instrument when it is scaled up that do not exist or have a very small impact in the smaller scale experiment. A well known example is the reduction in kindergarten class size in California in response to the findings of the Tennessee STAR experiment, which was less effective than expected because of an insufficient supply of good quality teachers.

All this means is that the vast majority of education production research (and other fields of educational and social research as well) needs to use non-experimental data – i.e. that collected from natural settings. So I now want now to turn to the vexed issue of recovering estimates of causal effects from data generated from natural settings. The crucial questions are:

(i)   Can it be done and if so how?
(ii)  If it can only be done with risk of unknown bias in the estimated effect sizes under what conditions is it worth doing?

Behind these questions lie the wishes of policy makers to have evaluations of policy effects either from a genuine desire to know if a particular policy is worth investing in or to legitimate policies with an appeal to pseudo-scientific evidence. Also with something at stake are the quantitative evaluators who seek customers for their specially honed skills.

Heckman (2000) has written an excellent paper on 'Causal parameters and policy analysis in economics', upon which I draw. He notes that where econometrics and statistics diverge is in the use of economic modelling for the analysis of causal effects. The major contributions of econometrics have been to:

- take from philosophy the idea that many models are consistent with the same data (the models are over-determined);
- show that causality is most fruitfully investigated by applying formal economic models.

Given the first point, which is general to the social sciences, the second one is crucial and distinctive of economics, which consists of a network of interrelated theories based on the assumption of rational utility-maximising decision makers. It is not only quantitative causal modellers who rely on these postulates but also those who, like Little (1998), seek causal explanations from understanding the workings of causal mechanisms, which are set in motion by the actions of individual agents responding to incentives, constraints and powers exerted by other agents and social institutions.

I want to try now to explain how economic modelling relates to causal explanation and identification using the education production function as an example. This will also, I hope, illustrate how misspecification of the model being estimated results in the diverse findings and controversies over their interpretation.

I will start with a very simple model in which the attainment of an individual student, A, depends on a set of different resource inputs, R, and family/personal variables, F, such as ability, gender and parental education. To simplify, I will talk in terms of a single R and a single F variable but these categories can equally well consist of a whole list (or vector) of specific resources (teachers, non-teaching staff, materials, buildings, etc.) and family and personal variables.[6]

$$A = f(R, F) \qquad\qquad 1(a)$$

A simple linear regression of this model would be:

$$A = a_o + a_1R + a_2F + e \qquad\qquad 1(b)$$

A is the dependent variable and it is endogenous, meaning a variable that depends on other variables in the model. R and F and any other variables on the right-hand side are referred to as independent variables or explanatory variables and $a_0$, $a_1$ and $a_2$ are coefficients or parameters to be estimated. The term e is a disturbance or error term; it reflects the assumption that A is not determined exactly by R and F but is stochastic or probabilistic. It is assumed that N observations are made and that each observation is drawn by keeping R and F fixed at some value and drawing the resulting value of A from a larger population.[7]

The objective is to obtain an estimate of the coefficient $a_1$ which is the effect of a change in R on attainment. This estimate should be unbiased and consistent. It is unbiased if when a large number of samples of size N were drawn and $a_1$ estimated each time then the average value of the estimate $a_1$ was the true population value. It is consistent if the estimate $a_1$ tends towards the true population value as sample size increases. There are a few other assumptions that the general linear regression model has to satisfy if the estimates are to be unbiased and consistent. (These are reproduced in the appendix.)

## Exogenously determined resources

An important assumption for $a_1$ to be a causal parameter is that R and F are exogenous. Exogenous variables are those that change only because of forces outside the model. Nothing within the model causes an exogenous variable to change. If R is exogenous then there is no correlation between it and the error term, e. In other words, the covariance between R and e is zero. Zero covariance between the independent variable, R, and the error term is an essential assumption for the estimator of $a_1$ to be unbiased and consistent. This is assumed in the commonly used statistical procedure known as ordinary least squares (OLS) for calculating the estimate of the parameter $a_1$. If the assumption is violated by the data then the estimates of the coefficients on the explanatory variables will be biased.

The attraction of the random controlled experiment is that R is by design exogenous. But if we are attempting to discover causal relations from naturally generated data, it is necessary to have sufficient variation in R – resources – to generate different and causally related levels of student attainment. Also, we need to control for differences in other variables – family background influences for example – by including them in the regression analysis. Here statistical control attempts to make up for the absence of random assignment of students to different amounts of resource. In the case of estimating school production functions from non-experimental data, we need schools to be differentially funded in order to generate sufficient variation in R. If we had a national funding formula then we would be unable to estimate an education production function for schools since there would in effect be no variation in per pupil funding that was not pre-determined by the factors that enter the national funding formula. Every school with the same value of factors that determine costs, like school size and proportion of pupils eligible for free school meals, would receive the same per pupil funding.

## Omitted variables

Even if resources and all the other variables included on the right hand side of the production function equation 1(a) are exogenously determined there may be unobserved variables (because we do not have data on them) that have been omitted from the model but do affect attainment. For example, home background factors, such as parents' interest in their child's education and pupils' personality attributes that influence their motivation to learn, are important factors affecting attainment. Data on these are not usually available for school effectiveness and education production function studies, however. If these unobserved variables vary randomly then they exert no systematic bias on the estimated effect of resources on learning outcomes. However, if they are correlated with resources then differences in the unobserved variables will be associated with differences in R and variations in both will cause changes in student outcomes. For example, if parents who take a great interest in their child's education so that their children attain well at school also select better resourced schools, then R and the error term will move together, i.e. the covariance will not be zero as required for an unbiased estimate of the causal effect of resources on outcomes. The estimated effect of R on attainment will be biased because part of it (either negative or positive) is due to the unobserved variables. Again, the attraction of random controlled experiments is that R (the treatment of additional resources) is manipulated exogenously as part of the research design and so is not correlated with unobserved variables that affect treatment.

## Efficiency

The production function is derived on the assumption that producers are efficient, i.e. that firms aim to maximise profits: to do so requires producing at minimum feasible cost. Hence firms will choose production methods that maximise profits. Translated to schools the analogy is a model in which school managers maximise student outcomes subject to the constraints of the technology that relates inputs to student outcomes, the prices of the different inputs and the school budget. This behaviour generates a series of observations of resource inputs and related educational outputs from which one wishes to be able to estimate the coefficients of the education production function.

The production function is usually assumed to take the form depicted in Figure 1, where for simplicity all resources are treated as if they are a single resource so that they can be represented along a single axis in a two dimensional diagram. [8] The production function in Figure 1 is a graphical representation of equation 1(b), $A = f(R, F)$, in which family resources are assumed fixed so that the relationship simplifies to one between resources on the horizontal axis and attainment on the vertical axis. The line representing the relationship between resources and attainment is non-linear. Its shape derives from the usual assumption of increasing and then diminishing marginal returns to additional resources. At some point adding one additional unit of resource increases output by less than did the previous unit of resource. If all schools are efficient, apart from some random variation, then the combination of resources and average student attainment (assumed to adjusted for pupils' prior attainment) of a set of schools will be scattered along the education production function as illustrated by the points in Figure 1.

If technology changes so that educational resources become more productive then the whole production function will shift upwards. Another adjustment would occur if the relative prices of inputs changes. (This cannot be shown on

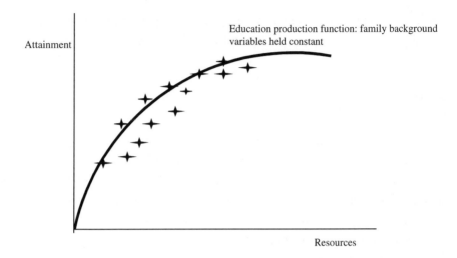

**Figure 1** Education production function (for given prices, technology and family background variables) when schools are efficient

this diagram because of the assumption of a single resource.) When relative input prices change, efficient producers substitute cheaper for more expensive inputs. For example, the government's remodelling of the school workforce encourages schools to increase the ratio of support staff to teachers in the face of a teacher shortage (ATL 2003). Given that schools operate efficiently, apart from some random variation, and receive different levels of exogenously determined resources, the observations of schools' attainment and resourcing levels would trace out an identifiable production function as illustrated in Figure 1. It is the underlying social processes, which we attempt to model that generate the data we observe. The research endeavour is to recover the model of the social processes from the data observed. The data may not reveal an education production function because schools do not behave efficiently as required for this relationship to be identifiable from empirical observation.

An alternative assumption about the behaviour of schools to that of efficiency (i.e. output maximisation subject to limited resources) is that schools are inefficient in their use of resources. There are several possible reasons for this. In the absence of competitive pressures schools do not have to maximise pupils' attainment in order to maintain enrolment and staff employment. Instead school managers and other staff can work less hard and/or spend less time obtaining the information needed to select the best available teaching and learning methods. This type of producer behaviour, which results in the costs of a given amount of output being higher than the feasible minimum, goes under the name of X-inefficiency (Leibenstein 1966; Levin 1997; Pritchett and Filmer 1999). If schools were X-inefficient then the observations of attainment paired with resourcing levels would not trace out a production function. This is illustrated in Figure 2, where schools are scattered randomly and there is no relationship between resources and attainment. School inefficiency is the rationale given by Hanushek for the apparent failure of education production studies to find sufficient evidence of positive and significant effects of resources on pupil outcomes.

An educationist's perspective on the absence of an observable positive association between the amount of resources and student achievement is that it is not resources but teacher–student interactions that determine learning, in the course of which resources are used with differing degrees of effectiveness.

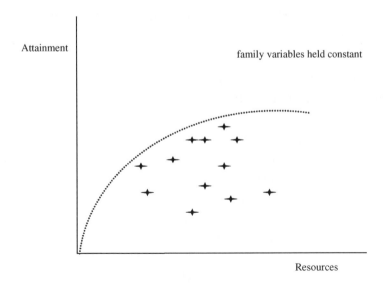

**Figure 2** Attainment–resource level observations when schools are X-inefficient

As Cohen *et al.* (2003) argue, resources do not cause learning – 'systems of instruction are the cause and resources the facilitators or inhibitors of learning'. However, from an economics perspective those instruction processes that do not achieve the highest possible student progress in learning from a given quantity of resources are inefficient compared to than those that do.

An alternative explanation for schools' actual or apparent inefficiency is absence of knowledge about the technology of learning – how to combine inputs in the best way to produce student learning. The education production function may exist and not be known or it may be so contingent on the actual circumstances of each school as not be generalisable.

These various conceptualisations of the education production imply that the institutional arrangements within which schools operate are very important because they determine the incentives to which managers, teachers, parents and pupils respond. These interactions determine the efficiency with which resources are used and the resulting outcomes for students, teachers and other interested parties.

## Endogeneity and the problem of identifying causal resource effects

So far I have only dealt with the supply side of the model, assuming that school resources are exogenously determined. On the demand side of the education market parents are making choices with respect to investing in their children's education. Parents spend their own time and also money in purchasing books, computers, extra-curricular activities and formal tuition. Parents exercise choice of school. So better educated and higher income parents may be more likely to choose well-resourced schools with good teachers. This means that the basic one-equation model outlined earlier has to be augmented by a further equation in which resources depend on family variables. The model is now:

$$A = f(R, F) \qquad 1(a)$$
$$R = g(F, Z) \qquad 2(a)$$

where R = the resources expended on an individual child depend on his/her family variables and also on some additional exogenous factor Z, such as the educational funding policies of the local education authority, given that these do not determine where the family decides to live. Resources are now partly endogenous because they depend on another variable in the model, the family variables. If we fit a single equation production function and obtain a positive estimate of $a_1$, the coefficient on R, some of this apparent effect of resources on attainment is due to the effect of the family variables. The resource variables are endogenous because an increase in school resources induces a change in family resource inputs. Therefore the assumption required for an unbiased and consistent estimator of $a_1$, that resources and the error term do not covary, is not met.

Another way in which resources can be endogenous through family choice is if parents respond to lower amounts of school resources by increasing their own inputs. As Todd and Wolpin (2003) point out, the effect of a reduction in class size that is identified by an experimental study is not necessarily the same as that which an education production function study using non-experimental data would identify. In an experimental study, the observed effect of small classes compared to large classes will include the effects of any offsetting behaviour by parents. The causal effect is the effect on attainment after all the responses to the treatment have worked their way through to attainment. Whereas the parameter that is of concern in an education production function is the effect of class size on attainment, keeping other variables constant. The effect of class size on attainment after allowing for participants' responses is the information that policy makers need.

In the UK the most important source of endogeneity for school resource variables is compensatory funding. LEA school funding formulae, while being required to allocate at least 75 per cent of LEA funding on the basis of age-weighted pupil numbers, also contain other elements for special educational needs and social disadvantage (Marsh 2002). This means that at school level attainment is negatively related to funding per pupil as illustrated in Figure 3, which plots school revenue per pupil taken from Section 52 outturn statements for 2001/02 against the percentage of students with 5 or more A\* to C grade passes at GCSE/GNVQ. The inverse relationship between a school's revenue per pupil and attainment is likely to be less pronounced at pupil level but will still exist given that low SES pupils are disproportionately concentrated in certain schools. Within schools also the allocation of resources to individual pupils is often related to the student's ability so that less able pupils are taught in smaller classes (see Iacovu 2002). When compensatory resourcing is practised, then an ordinary least squares regression of attainment on resources plus control variables will produce a downward biased estimator for resources and one which may also be negative.

I have restricted the example of endogeneity to a two-equation formal model (equations 1(a) and 2(a) above) since it is not necessary to write out additional equations to make the point that one can develop a more fully specified model of educational choice involving both the consumers and producers of education. Parents and children choose how much time and money to invest in education, where to live and which school to attend. Central and local governments

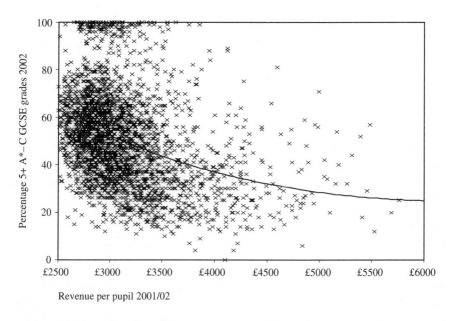

**Figure 3** Relationship between revenue per pupil and percentage of students obtaining 5 or more A*–C GCSE grades

decide on funding allocations in relation to indicators of attainment and social disadvantage. Governors, managers and teachers in schools make choices about how to use the resources within the school to best effect. This includes teachers deciding at which school to work in response to student and resourcing factors. Mayston (2002), for example, in a DfES commissioned report developed a 16-equation model of the demand and supply sides of the schools market with 12 endogenous and 4 exogenous variables. This kind of model specifies a set of causal mechanisms, which are set in motion by the utility maximising decisions of the various actors interacting with each other.

The problems revealed by focusing on the behaviours of economic agents that affect the relationship between resources and student outcomes can be examined using a small two-equation model. To simplify further I have written them in linear form. The model set out in terms of the initial equations in which both exogenous and endogenous variables appear on the right hand side is know as the **structural form**. Attainment depends on resources and an exogenous variable X, while resources depend on attainment and another exogenous variable Z. Resources are linked to attainment via such practices as compensatory funding and family choice of school.

$$A = a_0 + a_1 R + a_2 X \qquad\qquad 1(b)$$
$$R = b_0 + b_1 A + b_2 Z \qquad\qquad 2(b)$$

An OLS estimation of equation 1(b) will produced a biased and inconsistent estimate of $a_1$ because of the endogeneity of resources.

## Approaches to estimating parameters in equations that form part of a system of equations

So we have to recognise that the education production function is part of a system of equations that model the behaviour of consumers and producers in an education market. Consequently resources are likely to be endogenously related to student outcomes as well as outcomes being dependent on resources.

This means that studies using non-experimental data to estimate the causal effect of resources on student outcomes must take account of the endogeneity of resources. There are several approaches to this estimation problem, which I outline below.

### System methods

One approach is to estimate the whole model – that is all the equations together. Some use is made of this approach in school effectiveness research where some researchers apply a method known as structural equation modelling. It has been advocated, for example, for research on the effects of educational leadership on students' attainment (e.g. Hallinger and Heck 1998; Leithwood and Jantzi 2000; Mulford *et al.* 2004). It is only used to any extent by economists for macroeconomic modelling which is for forecasting purposes rather than investigating causality. The main reason economists are not keen on systems methods is that obtaining unbiased and consistent estimators is dependent on correctly specifying all the equations in the structural model. Structural equation models, while called causal path models, need to have the causal paths assumed prior to estimation. Then the covariances generated by the model are compared to those in the data to judge whether the model fits the data sufficiently well (Schumacker and Lomax 1996).

### Single-equation methods

Single-equation methods are therefore the most popular for the estimation of education production functions. There are several of these which are in many ways equivalent.

### Reduced form: indirect least squares

This method could be employed if one could solve the system of structural equations (which is specified as a system of linear simultaneous equations) by expressing each of the endogenous variables only in terms of the exogenous variables. The reduced form equations would look like:

$$A = r_{11} + r_{12}X + r_{13}Z + u_1 \qquad\qquad 3$$
$$R = r_{21} + r_{22}X + r_{23}Z + u_2 \qquad\qquad 4$$

The estimators of coefficients $r_{11}$ to $r_{23}$ would be unbiased and consistent given X and Z are exogenous.

The problem lies in getting back from the reduced form coefficients to the structural form coefficients: that is working out what are the values of $a_0$ to $b_3$ from the estimated values of $r_{11}$ to $r_{23}$. This is known as the **identification problem**.

A model is just-identified if one can obtain just one set of values for the structural coefficients that is consistent with the values of the reduced form coefficients. The condition for just identification applies to each of the equations of the structural model separately. Some equations can be just-identified and others not. The necessary condition for a structural equation in a model of M simultaneous equations to be exactly identified is that it must exclude M−1 variables in the model.[9] The conditions necessary for a structural equation to be just-identified and therefore to be able to use the reduced form estimators (a method known as indirect least squares) are rarely satisfied as they often imply restrictions on the structural equations that are not plausible. If it is not possible to identify the structural coefficients at all then it is not possible to estimate them because there is no solution to the system of structural equations. There are too few variables in the model relative to the number of equations.

However, if an equation is over-identified one can estimate it. In this case there is more than one possible set of values of the structural coefficients consistent with the values of the reduced form coefficients.

### Instrumental variables

An instrumental variable is an exogenous variable that varies with the endogenous explanatory variable (resources) but not with the dependent variable (attainment). The instrumental variable causes R (resources) to vary when it changes but is not itself a direct causal factor in the attainment equation. For an instrumental variable in an education production function study we need some exogenous factor that causes resourcing per student in schools to vary but which is independent of the endogenous factors such as family background and attainment. Resources can vary with the endogenous variables but part of the variation in resources must be due only to the variation in the exogenous variable.

Given Z is exogenous in equation 2(b) below, it causes R to vary but is not itself correlated with attainment because it is not present in the attainment equation 1(b). The variation in variable Z causes the resource function to shift along the production function – as shown in Figure 4. Each of the downward sloping lines is a resource function showing how the level of school resourcing depends inversely on student attainment, as it does when local authorities' funding formulae include an element of compensatory funding for social disadvantage. Each LEA has a different resource function depending on its average level of funding, which is higher in some LEAs than others. The set of LEA resource functions generate a number of data observations (combinations of A and R) where they intersect the production function and these data points trace out (i.e. identify) the production function.

$$A = a_0 + a_1R + a_2X \qquad \qquad 1(b)$$
$$R = b_0 + b_1A + b_2Z \qquad \qquad 2(b)$$

If there is a large number of different local education authorities, with different funding levels determined by local political factors, these provide an instrumental variable. To ensure that school resources are exogenous to home background and hence student attainment, residents must not choose where to live according to school funding policies. Local authority boundary changes would

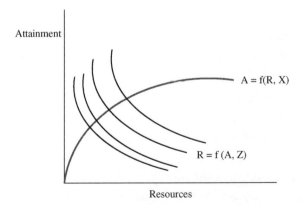

**Figure 4** An exogenous variable in the resource function enables identification of the education production function

create such an ideal situation for a few years. A good example of exogenous local school resources is South Africa during the apartheid period (Case and Deaton 1999) as Blacks had little choice over place of residence and expenditure per pupil varied regionally. Another source of an instrumental variable is in rules that keep classes at a prescribed maximum (Angrist and Lavy 1999). Class sizes in schools and hence resourcing per pupil are then dependent on the number of children in a year group.

Instrumental variables (IV) estimation involves regressing R (the endogenous explanatory variable) on Z (the instrument) and then replacing R in the production function equation by values of R predicted by Z. This is the exogenous variation in R. Several instrumental variables, if they have been found, would be used as regressors for R, resources. The movements in the instrumental variable(s) generate differences in school revenues per pupil that are unrelated to attainment or to the other family variables that are correlated with attainment. The IV generated movements in R do not therefore covary with the error term.

Instrumental variables are not a panacea. If they are not well correlated with the potentially endogenous explanatory variable, the variance of the resulting estimator will be high (Bound *et al.* 1995). Also, the instrument selected may be correlated with the dependent variable, which an IV should not be. In practice it is often difficult to find good instrumental variables, consequently the ones actually used in some studies do not satisfy the requirements for an IV.

It should also be borne in mind that an IV estimate comes from the impact of the endogenous explanatory variable on the dependent variable *for those in the sample affected by the instrument.* An example often given is the school leaving age IV, used in some studies for estimating the rate of return to a year of schooling (Angrist and Krueger 1991; Meghir and Palme 2001; Card 2001). Schooling is endogenous, so people use changes in the legal school leaving age as an instrument. Changes in the law ensure that individuals who would previously have left school at age 15 had to stay on school till 16. They had an extra year of schooling that was truly exogenous (i.e. determined by the law not their family background). This makes a good IV, in the sense that the instrument is highly correlated with the endogenous explanatory variable, in this case years of schooling, and not correlated with, say earnings. However, the law generally only affected those *who would have left school at age 15.* Thus using the law change as an IV gives a Local Area Treatment Effect estimate of the return to schooling for those who would previously have left school at age 15, rather than for the population as a whole.

## Quasi- and natural experiments

An alternative to random controlled trials is provided by quasi-experiments. Here, a policy intervention is tried on one group of people and the effect of the treatment on the intervention group for an outcome is compared with the same outcome variable for a control group which was not treated. However, the conditions for a RCT are not satisfied since the assignment of individuals to the treatment and control groups is not random. For example a policy such as the pilot for Educational Maintenance Allowances (Ashworth *et al.* 2001) can be considered quasi-experiments. The pilot National Literacy Strategy and Excellence in Cities (EiC) (Machin and McNally 2004; Machin *et al.* 2003) have also been evaluated as quasi-experiments. The treatment variable (e.g. being in an area selected for the education maintenance allowance pilot or for EiC) is the instrumental variable.

Natural experiments are similar to quasi-experiments but the term is usually reserved for policy or other exogenous changes which one group of people experiences and another does not (e.g. a change in the compulsory school leaving age) but which are not the result of a deliberate policy intervention experiment. In a natural experiment the people who experience an exogenous variation are not randomly assigned to it. In effect both quasi- and natural experiments can be experiments in every sense except without random assignment (Cook 1991).

The problem with both quasi- and natural experiments is to find a control group that can provide a sufficiently good counterfactual for the treatment group. The outcomes of the treatment group must not be biased relative to the control group because of the characteristics they possess that led them to be selected for treatment in the first place. The control group therefore needs to be selected from a larger population of non-treated so that they match as far as possible the treatment group in relation to the factors that determine selection into the treatment group. (There is a more extensive but basic explanation of this in

Baker (2000)). The matching criterion is the propensity score or the probability of being in the treatment group. The probability of being in the treatment group is first estimated using the observed characteristics of the treatment group. The control group is then selected on the same characteristics so that each treatment group member is matched to one or more persons in the control group who have the same or very similar probability of being selected for treatment but were not. The crucial assumption for matching using propensity scoring to remove selection bias is that selection can be explained by the observed variables and this may not be achieved. If selection is affected by unobserved variables then the control and treatment groups differ in ways that may bias the estimated treatment effect.

Another problem is that some treatment group members may have such specific characteristics that led them to be selected (e.g. highly deprived schools selected for EiC) that they cannot be matched with controls and have to be excluded from the evaluation. Then one has no estimate of the treatment effect for these schools as it may be different from the average effect on the schools included in the matched sample. To remove the effects on outcomes of unobserved variables the effects of which are constant over time, first differencing is recommended. This requires data on the treatment and control groups *before* the treatment was implemented and then for at least one period *after* the treatment has been received and had time to have an effect. The difference in outcomes for the treatment group between the start of treatment and the time when its effect is measured is compared with the difference in outcomes for the control group over the same period of time, controlling if necessary for other variables that affect outcomes. For example in the EiC evaluation (Machin *et al.* 2003) the difference in examination results of EiC schools the year before and in the years after being in the EiC programme are compared to the same differences in results for the control group.

## Causality as a property of the model

The really important point about causality, which the foregoing discussion should bring out, is that causality cannot be inferred from data alone. Evidence of causal relations and causal effects depends on analysing data through the imposition of a model. For economists the models should not be ad hoc but derived from economic theory, since this ensures consistency with received ideas of how economic agents behave and interact. Heckman's paper is notable in making it transparent that causality is a property of a model, that many models may explain the same data and that assumptions must be made to identify causal (i.e. structural) models. Therefore causal knowledge is conditional on both the modelling assumptions made and on the situations from which the data were generated. It follows that it is impossible to derive causal knowledge from the empirical data alone. Consequently 'economic theory as a framework for interpretation and synthesis is an inseparable part of good empirical research' (Heckman 2000). It is in the appeal to economic theory that econometrics has a distinctive approach to causality and one which is not so readily accepted amongst quantitative researchers with other discipline backgrounds (McKim and Turner 1997; Sobel 1998; Heckman 2000).

## Multilevel analysis

Another methodological issue is that education production function analysis involves different levels of analysis. Pupils are nested in classes or with teachers and these in turn are nested in schools. Further levels are local education authorities and finally countries if cross-national data sets like TIMMS (Third International Mathematics and Science Study) or PISA (Programme for International Student Assessment) are used. Pupils in the same class or school are expected to have some common effect exerted on their attainment. If this is the case then the error terms for pupils in the same class or school are correlated (known as serial correlation) and the variance of the error term for pupils in different classes/schools is likely to be different. This violates two assumptions required for OLS estimators to have minimum variance. Studies which either model the production function at pupil level or at school/state level and do not correct for serial correlation between the error terms have downward bias in the standard errors of the estimators. This leads to the risk of accepting estimators as statistically significant when they are not (Goldstein 1995). If the analysis is conducted at the aggregate level (e.g. at school or LEA level), it may be the case that statistical relationships between variables at an aggregate level can be quite different from those at the unit level (i.e. pupils) (Goldstein 1995) and can be biased (Hanushek 1996).

Multilevel modelling, to which the Institute of Education has made major contributions, including the development of the software package MLwiN (Rasbash *et al.* 2000; Goldstein 1995), enables one to estimate education production functions which correct for serial correlation and separate out the variance of attainment at the different levels. However, it does not include procedures for correcting for endogeneity through instrumental variables. It is possible to correct for the bias to standard errors arising from hierarchical data in other statistical packages.

## Functional form

Functional form refers to the mathematical form of the education production function equation. Linear regression estimates equations in a linear form but these can include a number of different specifications and need not be confined to the simple additive linear equation as are equations 1(b) and 2(b) above. A popular specification of the production function in economics is the multiplicative form (known as the Cobb-Douglas).

$$A = a_0 R^{a1} F^{a2} \qquad\qquad 1(c)$$

which is linearised by taking logarithms to give

$$\log A = \log a_0 + a_1 \log R + a_2 \log F \qquad\qquad 1(d)$$

Non-linear terms (polynomials or squares and cubes) of some of the variables can be included to reflect assumptions about rates of change, for example in the marginal product. Interaction terms can also be included. These are multiples of two variables, for example class size and ability, which test whether the effect of class size on attainment varies according to ability. Interaction terms often indicate that effects are not uniform but vary according to the characteristics of students. There is evidence in some studies that non-linear functional forms do matter for the estimates of resourcing effects and that this needs further exploration (Levačić and Vignoles 2002).

## Criteria for good quality studies of the education production function

I have now reviewed the main methodological issues in the statistical estimation of education production functions. We know what the problems are. But it is less clear whether a particular solution to any one of these problems, including ignoring the problem, is acceptable or valid or 'good enough'. There are no clear-cut criteria as to whether a model utilising non-experimental data has estimated causal parameters or suffers from other data and specification problems that undermine the credibility of the reported findings as causal.[10] The extent to which assumptions are made that enable unbiased and consistent causal parameters to be estimated and that these assumptions are realistic is a matter of judgement. Nevertheless, there are relatively clear criteria of what are very inadequately specified estimation models such as failure to address the endogeneity problem or to correct for serial correlation. In two reviews of education production function studies Anna Vignoles and I set out a list of criteria that good quality education production function studies should satisfy (Dolton *et al.* 2004; Levačić and Vignoles 2004).

1. The attainment data should be at pupil level, with controls for prior attainment or other measures of ability, pupil characteristics and home background. The resource data should be at school level at least (or class level) not LEA level. School context variables should be included. Including as large a range of variables as possible reduces the problem of bias due to omitted variables.

2. The endogeneity problem should be addressed, by using instrumental variables, for example for the resource variables. This includes

instruments for selection into natural experiments and for controlling for selection bias. Again, including a large number of relevant controls is another approach to reducing bias due to endogeneity (Dustmann *et al.* 2003).

3. Multilevel modelling or equivalent econometric techniques should be used to take account of the effects of serial correlation (due to the hierarchical nature of the data) on the standard errors of the estimating equations.

4. Functional forms as well as additive linearity should be tested.

## UK education production function studies: a review

In 1999/2000 the DfES Value for Money Unit commissioned a review of UK education production function studies (Vignoles *et al.* 2000). We found very few UK studies that met most of the criteria listed above. In the DfES report we included a number of weaker and generally older studies which had used LEA or school-level data and ignored the endogeneity problem, whereas in the shorter version published in Education Economics (Levačić and Vignoles 2002) we restricted the selection to the highest quality studies. I shall discuss these briefly as well as including a few more that have appeared since.

The criteria for selecting these studies are that they:

- use student-level data and have an outcome measure in terms of exam results, continuing in education, or wages;
- include at least one resource measure at school level such as expenditure per pupil, teacher–pupil ratio, class size;
- include prior attainment or family variables as controls;
- clearly identify the method of estimation and report estimated coefficients with standard errors/ t statistic;
- were mostly published in refereed journals or as discussion papers.

One cannot have a good study of the education production function (or other economic relationship) without good data. Governments and national agencies have a major role in creating good data sets. In this field I would like to acknowledge the work of the DfES in creating the National Pupil Database, a major component of which is the Pupil Level Annual Schools Census (PLASC), started in 2002. This provides attainment data at pupil level for all four key stages, plus pupils' gender, FSM eligibility, SEN status, ethnicity, EAL and home post code and a good number of school context and governance variables. Resourcing data are available at school level from the Annual Schools Census (ASC) and from Section 52 budget outturn statements. Great progress has been made in the quality of data and we should not forget this. The contrast of the quality of today's data with that of 25 years ago is striking. Hough's *A Study of School Costs*, (Hough 1981) was based on data that he had to personally collect from LEAs' files. His later attempt to relate school expenditure per pupil to student attainment (at school level) reported statistically insignificant relationships (Hough 1991).

The most frequently used dataset in good quality UK studies is the National Child Development Study (NCDS) of a sample of people born in one week in March 1958. This dataset includes good family background variables and tests of English and maths taken at 7 and 11 as well as subsequent examination results. However, school resourcing data are limited and the studies report on education production function relationships from the mid-1970s. A recent study on class size (Blatchford *et al.* 2002), funded by the DfES, collected its own data and another (Graddy and Stevens 2003) obtained data from the Independent Schools Information Service, but this has the drawback of being at school level.

The four studies we included in our 2002 review are Dearden *et al.* (2001), Dustmann *et al.* (2003), Feinstein and Symons (1999), and a single study published in Dolton and Vignoles (1999, 2000). Later studies summarised here are Blatchford *et al.* (2002), Graddy and Stevens (2003), Iacovou (2002). The studies use a variety of outcome measures: reading and maths scores at 7 and 11, reading and numeracy in the first year of school, O-level English and maths, post-16 participation in education, and wages at 23, 33 and 42 years of age. Between them these studies include class size, the pupil–teacher ratio and expenditure at LEA level as resource variables. The NCDS studies have a relatively large number of control variables for family background, prior attainment, gender, peer group and school type attended. Most of the studies rely on the inclusion of a large number of controls to cope with endogeneity and it is notable that resource effects in some of the studies disappear once the full set of controls is included. Iavocou uses the interaction between class size and school type as an instrumental variable and finds class size significant for reading at age 7 and 11. The main features of these six studies are summarised in Table 3 and the findings are summarised in Tables 4 and 5.[11]

Two of the studies (Iacovou and Blatchford *et al.*) found a positive effect of smaller class size on maths for young children, and the latter also reported a positive effect on reading. Dustmann *et al.* (2003) found a negative effect of higher pupil–teacher ratios (PTR) at 16 on the decision to stay on in full-time education but not a direct effect of the PTR on wages. However, participating in full time education post-16 did have a positive effect on wages at 33 and 42, indicating a small indirect effect of PTR on wages.[12] This indicates how estimating a reduced-form direct effect of school resources on earnings may fail to uncover the indirect effects mediated by other variables such as post-16 participation. Dolton and Vignoles found significant effects of the PTR on maths and English O-level results and earnings, and Dearden *et al.* on women's wages.

Some other UK studies using non-experimental data utilise school level data but do not address the endogeneity problem. Levačić and Jenkins (2004), in a study of pupil-level GCSE attainment in 2001 and school-type reported a negative and significant effect of higher pupil teacher–ratios but endogeneity was not corrected for other than by controls for prior attainment and school context variables, including free school meals. A reduction of 5.6 pupils per teacher was associated with an increase in 1 GCSE grade in 1 subject. Graddy and Stevens (2003) report positive effects on A-level results of smaller classes in English independent schools but the data is at school level and OLS estimation is used so that there may be bias due to endogeneity. The authors argue that because the sample is restricted to well-off parents, school fee levels and hence class size are not selected by parents according to their child's ability to succeed at A level.

Studies of natural experiments where a specific educational intervention requiring additional resourcing is evaluated tend to show positive effects

**Table 3** Student-level education production function studies: main features

| Authors | Output measure | School quality variables | Controls | Data | Statistical technique |
|---|---|---|---|---|---|
| Feinstein and Symons (1999) | EXAMS<br>1. English: highest grade attained in national exams in English up to age of 21 (has 8 categories)<br><br>2. Mathematical ability at 16 measured by NCDS test<br><br>3. Index of overall exam performance in all subjects | School type (single-sex, private, grammar, comprehensive, technical, secondary modern)<br><br>PTR at school level<br><br>Pupil in top stream<br>Not in top stream of streamed classes | PRIOR ATTAINMENT<br>NCDS 'ability' tests in maths at 11<br><br>FAMILY BACKGROUND<br>Parent interest variable;<br>Father in top or middle SES;<br>Father and mother stayed on at school;<br>No of older and younger siblings;<br>Father plays role in upbringing<br><br>PEER GROUP composite variable made up of:<br>% of children in class with fathers in non-manual occupations;<br>% of children in class only taking GCE exams;<br>% of children in class only taking CSE exams;<br>% of children in previous year's class taking who stayed on in education<br><br>ENVIRONMENT<br>local unemployment rate,<br>% of unskilled manual | NCDS<br><br>General population census | OLS and 2SLS<br><br>Monte Carlo simulations: sensitivity analysis to check effect of low correlation in 2SLS between instruments and endogenous variables |

| Study | Outcomes | School variables | Control variables | Data | Method |
|---|---|---|---|---|---|
| Dustmann et al. (2003) | EXAMS Number of 0 level and CSE grade 1 passes<br><br>DESTINATIONS Career choice (staying on, full and part-time training, labour market) | School type PTR at school level | PRIOR ATTAINMENT NCDS 'ability' tests in maths and English at 7 and 11. FAMILY BACKGROUND Family income; parents working; Parents' education; Child has separate room; No. of older and younger siblings; Parental interest; Parents want child to sit A levels/go to university ENVIRONMENT Local unemployment rate; % of unskilled manual workers | NCDS<br><br>General population census | OLS (ordered probit) Varied specifications. 2 stage estimates with instrumental variables |
| Dolton and Vignoles (1999, 2000) | EXAMS English and maths exam results at age 16: 1 = no qualifications in E or M; 2 = unclassified grade; 3 = CSE grade 3 or 4; 4 = 0 level grade D or E; 5 = 0 level C or CSE 1; 6 = 0 level grade A or B WAGES Log of gross hourly pay at age 33 for employed-males | School type English and maths class sizes (at 16); Square of class size; PTR at school level; School size; % students staying on; LEA expenditure per pupil; Teachers' salaries per pupil; PTR at LEA level; Child setted or streamed | PRIOR ATTAINMENT NCDS 'ability' tests in maths and English at 11. FAMILY BACKGROUND Gender; race; social class; Home ownership; Number of. siblings; Father present; Parental attitude to staying on at school PEER GROUP Attended school where: <20% pupils non-manual; >80% pupils non-manual | NCDS<br><br>LEA education statistics | OLS (ordered logit) Varied specifications |

*Continued*

35

**Table 3** Continued

| Authors | Output measure | School quality variables | Controls | Data | Statistical technique |
|---|---|---|---|---|---|
| Dearden *et al.* (2001) | EXAMS<br>Highest qualification obtained at school (A level, 5 + 0-level A-C or CSE 1, 1 + 0 level A-C or CSE 1, CSE 2-5, none)<br>Highest educational qualification obtained at age 23 or 33<br><br>WAGES<br>Wages at 23 and 33: hourly real gross wage rate in 1995 prices (of those in employment in 1981 and 1991) | School type<br>PTR at child's school at 11 & 16<br>LEA expenditure per pupil<br>LEA average teacher salaries in primary and secondary schools in 1969 and 1974 | PRIOR ATTAINMENT<br>NCDS 'ability' tests at 7 in verbal and maths ability<br><br>FAMILY BACKGROUND<br>Parental interest;<br>Father's social class;<br>Father's and mother's education;<br>In receipt of FSM;<br>Family financial difficulties;<br>No. of siblings and no. of older siblings<br><br>ENVIRONMENT<br>Regional school dummies (11);<br>Census (1971) SES variables of enumeration district in which child lived;<br>Social deprivation level of LEA (1971);<br>Size of LEA and its spending needs | NCDS<br><br>LEA education statistics<br><br>General population census | OLS ordered probit)<br><br>Varied specifications, including interaction terms between PTR and school type; and PTR and ability |

| | | | | | |
|---|---|---|---|---|---|
| Iacovou, M. (2002) | Reading and maths test scores aged 7, 11 and 16 | Class size, School size, Ability grouping, social class of peer group, LEA pupil-teacher ratio | FAMILY BACKGROUND Mother's and father's years of schooling, father's social class, parental interest in education, number of siblings, child's height and head circumference<br><br>POPULATION DENSITY Area dummies for Wales and London | NCDS | Instrumental vaiables: interaction between school size and school type |
| Blatchford and Goldstein (2002) | Reading Progress Test (Hodder and Stoughton) and a specially developed test of numeracy (maths) both administered by teachers | Class size in each term averaged over the school year Non-linear terms in class size included | Prior attainment (baseline) tests in literacy and maths, child's term of entry to school, age, gender and eligibility for free school meals | 368 classes in 220 English schools 5000–4500 children in Year 1 1996–7 | No attempt to control for endogeneity |

**Table 4** Summary of findings of student level studies on effect of resource variables on exam results

| | Class size | School PTR | Grouping & peer group | School type |
|---|---|---|---|---|
| Feinstein and Symons | Not included | Insignificant | Peer group=10.29<br>Top stream=7.57<br>Not top stream=−5.42 | Compared to comprehensive: coefficients for all exams:<br>grammar=7.56<br>sec. modern=−2.32<br>private is insignificant |
| Dustmann et al. | Not included | Significant when school type not included<br>Insignificant once school type included | | Significant. Compared to secondary modern coefficient on exam score:<br>Private=2.087<br>Grammar=1.916<br>Technical=1.13<br>Comprehensive=0.69 |
| Dolton and Vignoles | Significant but positively signed | Significant:<br>Maths score co-efficient=−0.091; English scorecoefficient=−0.068 | | Maths/English coefficients compared to comprehensive private=1.168 (M): 0.882(E)<br>grammar=0.585 (M); 0.886 (E)<br>sec. modern=−0.076 (M): −0.193 (E) |
| Dearden et al. | Not included | Not significant except for negative effect on men attending secondary moderns and lower ability women | | Men: grammar and private school has significant and positive effect, secondary modern negative effect.<br>Women: girls' school had significant positive effect |

| | | | |
|---|---|---|---|
| Iacovou (2002) | Significant and negative for reading. 8 fewer pupils increases score by.=0.29 of standard error. Insignificant for maths | Not included | Coefficients: top stream = 0.439 middle stream =0.166; bottom stream =−0.687 |
| | | | Infant school adds 0.128 of standard error to reading score |
| Blatchford and Goldstein (2002) | Decrease in class size of 10, at sizes below 25, associated with a gain of 1-year in achievement of low attainers; 5 months for other pupils | No effect of other adults in the class room | |

**Table 5** Summary of findings of student level studies on effect of resource variables on other outcomes

| | Dustman et al. STAYING ON | Dolton and Vignoles WAGES AT 33 | Dearden et al. WAGES AT 23 & 33 |
|---|---|---|---|
| Class size[a] | Not included | Insignificant in full specification | Not included |
| School PTR | Significant. Decrease in PTR by 1 sd. increases probability of staying on at school by 4% points. Stronger for boys. Staying on has positive effect on wages at 33 & 42 | Not significant once control for ability, qualifications, personal factors and experience | Negative and significant effect on wages at 33 for women attending grammar schools |
| LEA PTR | Not included | Insignificant | Not included |
| LEA spending per pupil | Not included | Insignificant | 10% increase in average secondary teachers' salary per pupil leads to 10% higher male wages at 23. 10% increase in LEA secondary school expenditure per pupil leads to 3.1% higher female wages at 23 |
| School type | Grammar/private school increases staying on by 16/19 percentage points | Significant | Private school has 9% impact on male wages at 33. Has positive impact on female wages at 33 |

*Source:* Levačić and Vignoles, 2002.
*Note:*
[a] Dustmann *et al* use the pupil teacher ratio at the school attended and call this class size. These are different variables since for a given pupil teacher ratio class size at school level varies directly with the amount of non-contact time teachers.

on learning of the intervention and hence of the additional resources. Two studies of 'natural experiments' make use of PLASC (Machin and McNally 2004; Machin *et al.* 2003). The latter found a small effect of Excellence in Cities on KS3 results for maths and English. There was more impact on boys of lower ability. The higher the allocations of additional funding which schools received the more pronounced the impact on boys' KS3 maths, but not on English. These results are initial findings: the impact on attainment may be greater over a longer period of time. An evaluation of the pilot phase of the national literacy strategy (Machin and McNally 2004) indicates that this had positive effects on children's KS2 results and was a cost-effective intervention.

However, there are also weak English production function studies, some of which may have been commissioned with a view to providing supportive evidence for investing in school resources. An example is a DfES-commissioned study relating schools' capital spending in 1993–5 to attainment at school level in 1995–9, controlling for school type, percentage of students eligible for FSM and region (PriceWaterhouseCoopers 2000). The study uses aggregated data and claims that multivariate analysis tests a causal relationship. It makes no mention of the possible endogeneity between school attainment, growth in pupil roll and capital investment. The study reports that 'capital spending has a positive and significant impact on attainment at KS1 and KS3' but is 'relatively weak'. The media interpretation was somewhat different!

> Research from the Department for Education and Employment, published this week, showed it is vital that schools be well maintained and well-equipped if they are to raise standards.
>
> (*Times Educational Supplement 2001*)

The pressure to demonstrate accountability for public money by showing causal links between spending and pupil attainment can have the undesirable consequence of devoting resources to the production of evidence that, because of the nature of the data or the estimation techniques used, is of dubious validity. However, the bulk of DfES-commissioned research, including that on the economics of education, is of much better quality and takes a long-term perspective.

# Education production function findings for developing countries

Education production function theory and methodological issues with respect to its estimation apply equally well to developing countries but the enormous difference in the level and variability of resourcing of schools means that empirical relationships between student outcomes and marginal changes in resourcing will be different. All the evidence I have discussed so far applies to developed countries, where resourcing levels are comparatively high and, in most countries, do not vary greatly between schools of similar size and social composition. Many of the studies of the impact of school resources on outcomes in developing countries have stemmed from World Bank funded projects, data collection and research.

The importance of large disparities in per student resourcing and the absence of school choice for generating data that identify an education production function are evident in a study of South Africa by Case and Deaton (1999). Under the Apartheid system, Blacks had very limited residential and school choices. This reduces considerably the 'selection bias problem' that bedevils EFP research in developed countries, where better off parents are more likely to choose well resourced schools or education authorities practise compensatory funding. There were also large differences in the pupil–teacher ratios between Black schools – much larger than the differences observed even in the US. Using data from the 1996 South African census and two national surveys of school inputs, the study found that the size of the pupil–teacher ratio in the district where a person attended school had a significant and negative effect on the return to education of Black men. It was not significant for women, who have discontinuous employment because of child-rearing responsibilities, which affect their wages.

Schools in developing countries are particularly badly resourced relative to those in developed countries with respect to learning materials and school facilities.[13] Pritchett and Filmer (1999) present an interesting argument, backed up with empirical evidence from a range of studies, that there is a misallocation of resources in developing countries towards excessive expenditure on teachers and insufficient expenditure on physical inputs. The supporting evidence is the preponderance of findings that the marginal product of additional physical inputs is much greater than that of teacher salaries or class size. For example, a review of developing country EPF studies by Fuller and Clarke (1994), reproduced in Table 6, showed a greater proportion of studies with significant effects for physical inputs than for teacher inputs.

A study using non-experimental data from Ghana and correcting for selection bias (Glewwe and Jacoby 1994) found that school inputs do enhance learning but that not all types were statistically significant. Conditions of classrooms (leaking and unusable classrooms) had a strong effect on reading and mathematics scores for middle-school pupils. Among instructional resources only blackboards were significant for maths and reading attainment. Teacher experience and length of schooling of teachers had no effect.

An extensive evaluation of a primary school development project in rural Northeast Brazil in the 1980s by Harbison and Hanushek (1992) found that additional physical resources were generally more cost-effective than teacher inputs, though both had positive effects, as shown in Table 7. Higher teacher salaries were the least cost-effective.

**Table 6** Summary from Fuller and Clarke (1994) of positive and significant resource effects on student achievement

|  | Number of studies | Positive and significant effects | Confirmation of findings percentage |
|---|---|---|---|
| **Primary schools** | | | |
| Teachers' salary | 11 | 4 | 36.4 |
| Teacher pupil ratio | 26 | 9 | 34.6 |
| Teachers' education | 18 | 9 | 50 |
| Teachers' experience | 23 | 13 | 56.5 |
| Class instruction time | 17 | 15 | 88.2 |
| Frequency of homework | 11 | 9 | 82 |
| School library | 18 | 16 | 89 |
| School textbooks | 26 | 19 | 73 |
| **Secondary schools** | | | |
| Teachers' salary | 11 | 2 | 18 |
| Teacher pupil ratio | 22 | 2 | 9 |
| Teachers' experience | 12 | 1 | 8.3 |
| Class instruction time | 16 | 12 | 75 |
| School textbooks | 13 | 7 | 54 |

**Table 7** Cost effectiveness ratios for additional spending on primary education in rural Northeast Brazil (achievement gain per US dollar spent)

| Input | Portuguese | Mathematics |
|---|---|---|
| Hardware (water, bookcase, teacher table, pupil chair, desk, 2 classrooms, large room, director's room, kitchen, toilet, store cupboard) | 0.37 | 0.39 |
| Textbook usage | 3.73 | 2.50 |
| Writing materials | 1.3 | 1.52 |
| Alternative teacher education strategies | | |
| Curso de Qualificacao (a remedial programme for teachers who did not complete 8 grades of primary school) | 0.13 | 0.27 |
| Logos (a programme to give teachers with complete primary education a qualification equivalent to 3 years secondary schooling) | 0.91 | 0.75 |
| 4 years primary school education | 0.93 | 1.45 |
| 3 years secondary school education | 0.28 | 0.43 |
| Teacher salary | 0.11 | 0.11 |

*Source:* Harbison and Hanushek (1992) Table 6.2, p. 138.
*Note:* The outcomes are test scores in Portuguese and mathematics for second grade pupils averaged over the years 1981, 1983 and 1985.

An evaluation of the Primary Education Quality Improvement Project (PEQIP) in Indonesia from 1992–7 produced mixed results (Creemers and Werf 2000). Some of the four interventions listed in Table 8 had positive cost-effectiveness ratios for additional expenditure compared to non-project schools for some subjects, while others were negative. Community participation appeared to be the most and management development the least cost-effective interventions. In contrast, a school-improvement project in Sri Lanka organised and funded by the Swedish International Development Agency in socially dis-advantaged communities, which upgraded school facilities and provided teacher development and parent education, was found to have consistently positive effects on language and mathematics attainment compared to similar non-project schools (Gunasekara and Levačić 2004).

Two studies in (Baker 2000) of randomised experiments with additional physical resources were found to have positive effects on student outcomes. Providing textbooks and radio lessons increased primary pupils' attainment quite substantially in Nicaragua. In the Philippines providing multilevel learning

**Table 8** Effect sizes, unit costs of inputs, and cost-effectiveness ratios for four PEQIP interventions

| Intervention | Unit cost | Bahasa Indonesia | | Maths | | Science | |
|---|---|---|---|---|---|---|---|
| | | Effect size | Cost Effectiveness ratio | Effect size | Cost Effectiveness ratio | Effect size | Cost Effectiveness ratio |
| Teacher development | 67 | −.22 | −.0033 | 0.13 | .0019 | .3 | .0045 |
| Management | 20 | −.10 | −0055 | 0.18 | .0090 | 0 | 0 |
| Books and materials | 36 | 0.15 | 0.0042 | 0.10 | .0028 | −.10 | −.0028 |
| Community Participation | 4 | 0.27 | 0.0670 | 0.18 | 0.0450 | 0.18 | .0450 |

*Source:* Creemers and Werf (2000).
*Note:* Effect size is the gain in achievement in project schools compared with non-project schools measured in standard deviation of test score. Cost effectiveness is effect size per 100 rupiah.

materials for primary pupils in low-income municipalities reduced dropping out in grades 1–6 and improved test scores, especially when combined with a programme to enhance parent–school partnerships. Providing free school lunches had little effect on outcomes.

There is considerable evidence from developing country contexts that physical inputs have a positive impact on student outcomes, whereas that for positive effects on student outcomes of increased spending on teachers is rarer. Pritchett and Filmer (1999) attribute this to producer capture by teacher interests. This is a good example of received theory being used to interpret data. Appealing to public choice theory that public sector employees maximise their utility in terms of pay, conditions or job security rather than in terms of services to clients, it is argued that teacher inputs are over-employed and physical inputs under-used compared to the efficient combination of these inputs. Pritchett and Filmer offer some evidence that decentralisation of resource decisions is associated with greater productivity. Evidence for the marginal productivity of additional physical resources in developed countries is much less prevalent. This may not be because of less producer capture but because of the much greater quantity and quality of physical resources, so that their marginal productivity is much lower compared to additional staff than is the case in developing countries.

Because of the very different levels of resourcing in developing and developed countries one would expect to find different estimations of the effects of resources on student outcomes. But, in both contexts, the empirical evidence is marked by a consistent theme that resource usage in schools is often inefficient and that policy solutions should encompass creating appropriate incentives for promoting efficiency as well as, where warranted, additional resources.

## Current work: resourcing and attainment at KS3

In the final section of this lecture I would like to report briefly work at the Institute of Education on education production function analysis. Since 2000 the Value for Money Unit at the DfES has funded various studies on the education production function for English schools. The first study was a literature review (Vignoles *et al.*, 2000), the second an examination of methodology and data sources (Levačić and Feinstein, 2001) and the third a pilot study to test out the research design for collecting the additional data not already routinely collected (PriceWaterhouseCoopers and Institute of Education, 2003). The pilot study was designed to collect data on school climate and classroom processes as well as on resources.

The fourth study funded by the Value for Money Unit is on the relationship between school resources and pupil attainment at Key Stage 3. This uses pupil level attainment data at Key Stage 3 in English, maths and science for 2003 and pupils' prior attainment at KS2 in 2000. PLASC provides us with pupil characteristics as listed above. The study includes school type, governance and context variables (such as % FSM, % SEN, % low-achieving ethnic groups). We have used pupils' home post-codes to link to census data on the output area, which gives indicators of socio-economic status for the immediate neighbourhood of the pupils. These indicators can be used as proxies for the students' family background or as neighbourhood indicators. The resourcing variables are at school level - expenditure per student, the pupil teacher ratio and pupil-non-teaching staff ratio. The resourcing variables are available for all three years the students have been at secondary school.

Two instrumental variables for the resourcing variables have been used both singly and together – the political party in control of the authority in the year of budget setting and school size, since both are correlated with resourcing per pupil but are not directly related to attainment. We have found positive statistically significant effects on maths and science attainment at KS3 of expenditure per pupil and significant negative effects for the pupil teacher ratio. However the effects of resourcing per pupil on English attainment were insignificant. We found no evidence of a significant and correctly signed effects on attainment for pupils per non-teaching-staff. The effects of resources though positive are small, though up to 10 times larger for estimates from instrumental variables regressions than from ordinary least squares. The summary results for the resource variables are shown in Table 9. Resource effects were higher for pupils eligible for free school meals than those not eligible. (The full results for science are given in Table A1 in the Appendix.)

**Table 9** Effect of school resources on pupil attainment at Key Stage 3

| Variable | Instrumental Variables (2SLS) | | |
| --- | --- | --- | --- |
| | Coefficient | t Stat | $p > \|t\|$ |
| *KS3 Mathematics* | | | |
| Expenditure per pupil | **0.00038** | 2.62 | 0.009 |
| Pupil teacher ratio | **−0.09791** | −2.48 | 0.013 |
| Pupils per non teaching staff | 0.00021 | 0.64 | 0.521 |
| *KS3 Science* | | | |
| Expenditure per pupil | **0.00036** | 2.61 | 0.009 |
| Pupil teacher ratio | **−0.12340** | −2.87 | 0.004 |
| Pupils per non teaching staff | 0.00039 | 1.09 | 0.277 |
| *KS3 English* | | | |
| Expenditure per pupil | −0.00019 | −0.71 | 0.475 |
| Pupil teacher ratio | −0.05438 | −0.80 | 0.421 |
| Pupils per non teaching staff | **0.00150** | 2.72 | 0.007 |

*Source:* Levačić *et al* (2004).
*Note:* Figures in bold are statistically significant at 5%.

# Conclusions

The questions posed by education production function research are important ones. In particular for improving resource allocation decisions we need better knowledge of the following:

- Does a marginal increase in overall spending at particular stages of education raises attainment and if so, by how much?
- How does an increase in expenditure on the educational provision of specific groups of students affects their outcomes: is spending more effective when targeted at some kinds of pupils than at others?
- How does changing the mix of resources affects students' learning outcomes?
- Does additional expenditure on some subjects produce greater gains than for others?
- What are the characteristics of effective teachers and how much value do these characteristics command on the labour market?

Research on these questions has been hampered by the difficulty of tackling the endogeneity problem when data are inadequate. Increasingly, studies that use instrumental variables are producing correctly signed and significant resource effects. The quality of data has improved vastly in the UK, where the NCDS is no longer the only data source. The Pupil Level Annual Schools Census (PLASC) and Section 52 statements now provide good pupil level data and some school level data.

With improved data progress is now being made, as in the IoE study reported above. Using instrumental variables methods, we have found statistically significant and correctly signed, though small, resource effects of expenditure per pupil and the pupil-teacher ratio for maths and science attainment at KS3. But to progress in the range of questions we can address we require good data at class and teacher level for representative samples of schools, which PLASC does not provide.

The endogeneity problem can be avoided if exogenous variation in resourcing is created through experimentation with specific targeted increases in resources and random assignment of pupils to different levels of resource. Evaluations of quasi and natural experiments tend to more frequently produce confirmatory results for the impact of resources on learning outcomes when used in specific ways (Cohen et al. 2003).

We need more evaluations of increases in specific resources conducted under experimental conditions. For example, the government is pressing ahead with national adoption of 'work force remodelling' with no evidence of the impact that non-teaching staff have on student learning. What little evidence we have suggests that they have no impact. The STAR studies reported no effect of teaching assistants. This finding was repeated by Muijs and Reynolds (2002), in an experimental study of English primary school mathematics teaching which reported no effect on maths attainment of the use of teaching assistants.

Even where there are controls but assignment is not random, it may be difficult to match treated cases with controls with the same probabilities of being selected. For example, we are just starting work at the Institute of Education on an evaluation of the extension of interactive white boards in London secondary schools. Schools have been allocated money to equip at least one core subject department. The controls are therefore the subject departments that do not get allocated interactive boards as part of the scheme. Instead of the interactive boards being randomly allocated to the three core subject departments, schools chose which department was fully equipped. One expects that departments that were more likely to be successful in utilising interactive boards were selected, thus biasing upwards the treatment effect measured by comparing the exam results of treatment and control departments. The evaluation research design would have been more robust had the departments been selected randomly for being fully equipped with interactive white boards.

Those who advocate justifying policies by evidence of their cost-effectiveness need to be more aware of the distortions in the evidence created that this instance can bring about. The effect of the Treasury's insistence on spending departments like the DfES demonstrating value of money from programmes leads to a desperate search for causal evidence. Some evaluation specifications from government departments and non-governmental agencies seek evidence of causal impact from projects that have been set up in such away that a causal impact cannot be identified. Another response is to commission correlational studies and use these as evidence of causal impact.

Generally there is a very loose usage of terms like 'effect', 'impact' 'leads to', etc. in educational research and its discussion, with insufficient awareness of the caveats and conditions that have to be attached to causal interpretations. How far we can go in making causal inferences is not clear-cut by any means. At one end of the spectrum are the causal purists who only accept as causal evidence that which comes from RCTs or perhaps well-matched quasi- and natural experiments. At the other extreme are those who totally reject the attempt to accumulate evidence on what works for the purposes of policy manipulation.

As a pragmatist, I occupy the difficult ground between these two extremes. If policy is to be informed by as good evidence as we can get at any particular time and place, then it is very limiting to be purist and unhelpful to reject making causal inferences except when RTCs have been conducted. More can and should be done to urge policy makers to set up their policies so that they can be better evaluated via experimental designs. Even so, there will remain many areas where causal inferences have to be made from data from natural settings. In doing this researchers need to be more explicit that causal interpretations are derived by researchers interacting between the data and models of the processes by which they believe that the data were generated. Knowledge of causal relations in the social sciences is conjectural and conditional: it is subject to revision as both as our research methods develop and social processes change.

# Appendix

## Assumptions of the classical general linear model for unbiased and consistent estimators

$$Y = a_0 + a_1 X_1 + a_2 X_2 + e$$

1. The estimation equation is linear (i.e. $a_1$ is the effect of a change in $X_1$ on Y, with all other independent variables held constant)
2. Expected value of e (i.e. the mean value) is zero

$$E(e_i) = 0$$

3. The variance of the error term is constant

$$\text{Var}(e_i) = k \text{ for all } i$$

4. The covariance of the error term is zero

$$E(e_i, e_j) = 0 \text{ for all } i, j \text{ where } i \text{ does not equal } j$$

5. Observations on independent variables in repeated samples can be considered fixed.
6. There are more observations than independent variables and there is no exact linear relationship between any two independent variables.

Assumptions 3 and 4 do not hold in hierarchically structured data when the dependent variable is affected by the group to which the case belongs. Multilevel models avoid this problem.

Endogeneity undermines assumption 5 since the value of the dependent variable affects the variables defined to independent.

This above is explained further in Kennedy (1998).

Gujurati (1995) explains clearly that estimation equations are validly fitted for data derived from the whole population (population regression function) or from a sample of the population, which is more usual. Because the underlying model of a social process is assumed stochastic, a given set of values of the independent variables drawn for individuals or cases from the population have different values of the dependent variable. The estimated regression equation predicts the mean value of dependent variable, the average value of the error term being zero.

**Table A1** Regression of KS3 Science 2003 (IV using political variable instruments) including effect of expenditure peinuedr pupil

| Dependent variable: K3 science | Coef. | t statistic | stat significant |
|---|---|---|---|
| Expenditure per pupil (averaged over 3 years) | 0.0004 | 2.61 | *** |
| Female | −0.1171 | −55.90 | *** |
| Age (days from 1 Sept 1 1989) | 0.0003 | 33.10 | *** |
| SEN Action/Action Plus | −0.1473 | −27.84 | *** |
| SEN Statement | −0.0512 | −4.03 | *** |
| Eligible for FSM | −0.0932 | −27.81 | *** |
| *Ethnicity (base, white)* | | | |
| Asian, Indian | 0.0182 | 1.83 | * |
| Asian, Pakistani/Bangladeshi | −0.0587 | −4.77 | *** |
| Asian, other | 0.1094 | 6.76 | *** |
| Black | −0.0159 | −1.83 | * |
| Chinese | 0.1593 | 9.79 | *** |
| Mixed Ethnicity | −0.0012 | −0.16 | |
| First language not English | 0.0673 | 7.37 | *** |
| Key stage 2 total | −0.0143 | −2.06 | ** |
| Key stage 2 total squared | 0.0167 | 63.92 | *** |
| *School Variables:* | | | |
| School has sixth form | −0.0273 | −2.60 | *** |
| Stat lowest age 12 | −0.0077 | −0.31 | |
| Stat lowest age 13 | −0.0027 | −0.10 | |

*Continued*

**Table A1** Continued

| | | | |
|---|---|---|---|
| *Gender of school (base, mixed)* | | | |
| Boys' school | 0.0003 | 0.02 | |
| Girls' school | 0.1240 | 8.11 | *** |
| *Type of school (base, comprehensive)* | | | |
| Grammar school | 0.1138 | 7.01 | *** |
| Secondary modern school | 0.0239 | 1.48 | |
| Other type of school | 0.0003 | 0.01 | |
| *Religious denomination of school (base,* | | | |
| *non-denominational)* | | | |
| Roman Catholic | 0.0013 | 0.11 | |
| Church of England | 0.0211 | 1.50 | |
| Other Christian | −0.0643 | −1.44 | |
| Jewish | 0.0491 | 0.34 | |
| Per cent eligible for FSM in school | −0.0150 | −6.75 | *** |
| Per cent eligible for FSM squared | 0.0001 | 4.31 | *** |
| Per cent AEN in school | 0.0012 | 2.96 | *** |
| Specialist school | 0.0211 | 3.27 | *** |
| Special measures | −0.1443 | −3.88 | *** |
| EIC or EAZ | 0.0111 | 0.68 | |
| Beacon school | 0.0296 | 2.40 | ** |
| Leading Edge Partnership | −0.0082 | −0.45 | |
| Leadership incentive grants | −0.0709 | −3.38 | *** |
| Teachers' pay ratio (averaged) | 0.0673 | 1.31 | |
| Urban local authority district | −0.0249 | −2.82 | *** |
| Capacity Utilisation (averaged) | 0.1567 | 2.63 | *** |
| *Census variables:* | | | |
| Proportion Unemployed | −0.4031 | −5.13 | *** |
| Proportion Black Ethnicity | −0.0592 | −1.09 | |
| Proportion Chinese Ethnicity | −0.6186 | −4.10 | *** |
| Proportion Pakistani/Bangladeshi Ethnicity | −0.2314 | −7.47 | *** |
| Proportion Indian Ethnicity | −0.0061 | −0.15 | |
| Proportion Lone Parent Households | −0.1771 | −11.23 | *** |
| Proportion NVQ Level 1 or less | −0.3447 | −18.31 | *** |
| Constant | 1.8871 | 4.93 | *** |
| Obs | 433699 | | |
| $F_{(46, 2982)}$ | 7031.92 | | |

*Source:* Levačić et al. (2004)

*Notes:*

*** significant at 1%

** significant at 5%

* significant at 10%

## Notes

1 Times Educational Supplement 16 October 1987.
2 Before 2003 known as Education Standard Spending Assessment.
3 Another technique, data envelopment analysis, is used to calculate the efficiency of producer units and can accommodate multiple inputs and outputs (see Worthington, A.C. 2001: 245–68.)
4 Often economists distinguish between outputs (the immediate effects of schools on attainment, skills and behaviour) and outcomes (longer term effects that occur in adult life). Here I am using the two words interchangeably.
5 The counterfactual definition of causality is derived from J.S. Mill's A *System of Logic.*
6 In mathematical notation upper case notation, such as A and R, refer to a vector of variables (i.e. a list). Here, for simplicity, I am assuming just one type of A, R or F variable.
7 N may if data allow be the same size as the population. See Gujarati 1995: ch. 2.
8 If there are two or more inputs one can assume they are used in given proportions to each other which depend on their relative prices.
9 The sufficient condition for a structural equation to be just-identified is that the number of excluded exogenous variables is equal to the number of endogenous variables in the equation minus 1 (Gujarati 1995).
10 'No successful mechanical algorithm for discovering causal or structural models has yet been produced' (Heckman 2000: 89).
11 The tables are updated from Levačić and Vignoles (2002).
12 However, Dustmann *et al.*'s rough estimates of the impact of 1 less pupil per teacher on the subsequent increase in the present value of lifetime income suggest that the additional cost in teacher salaries would exceed the benefit. This of course assumes that wages are the only benefit of lower PTRs.
13 This also applies to European transition economies, where pupil–teacher ratios are quite low, but facilities are generally very poor.

## References

Angrist, G.D. and Krueger, A. (1991) 'Does compulsory school attendance affect earnings?' *Quarterly Journal of Economics,* 106, 6, 970–1014.
Angrist, J. and Lavy, V. (1999) 'Using Maimondes' rule to estimate the effects of class size on scholastic achievement'. *Quarterly Journal of Economics,* 114, 2, 533–75.

Ashworth, K., Hardman, J., Liu, W.-C., Maguire, S., Middleton, S., Dearden, L., Emmerson, C., Frayne, C., Goodman, A., Ichimura, H. and Meghir, C. (2001) *Education Maintenance Allowance: the first year: a quantitative evaluation.* DfES Research Report RB257. London: DfES.

ATL, DfES, GMDB, NHAT, NASUWT, NEOT, PAT, SHA, TGWU, UNISON and WAG (2003) *Raising Standards and Tackling Work Load: A national agreement.* Online. Available *http://www.gmb.org.uk/docs/pdfs/agreement-final.pdf* accessed 12 October 2004.

Baker, J. L. (ed.) (2000) *Evaluating the Impact of Development Projects on Poverty: A handbook for practitioners.* Washington, DC: World Bank.

Betts, J. (1996) 'Is there a link between school inputs and earnings? Fresh scrutiny of an old literature'. In G. Burtless (ed.) *Does Money Matter? The Effect of School Resources on Student Achievement and Adult Success.* Washington, DC: Brookings Institution.

Blatchford, P., Goldstein, H., Martin, C. and Browne, W. (2002) 'A study of the class size effects in English school reception year classes'. *British Educational Research Journal,* 28, 2, 169–85.

Bound, J., Jaeger, D.A. and Baker, R.M. (1995) 'Problems with instrumental variables estimation when the correlation between the instruments and the endogenous variable is weak'. *Journal of the American Statistical Association,* 90, 430, 443–51.

Burtless, G. (ed.) (1996) *Does Money Matter? The effect of school resources on student achievement and adult success.* Washington, DC: Brookings Institution.

Card, D. (2001) 'Estimating the return to schooling: progress on some persistent econometric problems'. *Econometrica,* 69, 5, 1127–60.

Card, D. and Krueger, A. (1996) 'Labour market effects of school quality: theory and evidence'. In G. Burtless (ed.) *Does Money Matter? The effect of school resources on student achievement and adult success.* Washington, DC: Brookings Institution.

Case, A. and Deaton, A. (1999) 'School inputs and educational outcomes in South Africa'. *Quarterly Journal of Economics,* CVIV, 1047–84.

Cohen, D., Raudenbush, S.W. and Ball, D.L. (2003) 'Resources, instruction and research'. *Educational Evaluation and Policy Analysis,* 25, 2, 119–42.

Coleman, J.S., Campbell, E.Q., Hobson, C.J., McPartland, J., Mood, A.M., Weinfeld, F.D. and York, R.L. (1966) *Equality of Educational Opportunity.* Washington, DC: Government Printing Office.

Cook, T. (1991) 'Clarifying the warrant for generalised causal inferences in quasi-experimentation'. In M.W. McLaughlin and D.C. Phillips (eds), *Evaluation and Education at a Quarter Century Part II.* Chicago: University of Chicago Press, 115–44.

Creemers, B. and Werf, G.V. (2000) 'Economic viewpoints in educational effectiveness: cost-effectiveness analysis of an educational improvement project'. *School Effectiveness and School Improvement*, 11, 3, 361–84.

Dearden, L., Ferri, J. and Meghir, C. (2001) 'The effects of school quality on educational attainment and wages'. *Review of Economics and Statistics*, 84, 1, 1–20.

Dewey, J., Husted, T.A. and Kenny, L.W. (2000) 'The ineffectiveness of school inputs: a product of misspecification'. *Economics of Education Review*, 19, 1, 27–45.

DfES (2002) *Departmental Investment Strategy 2003–06*. Online. Available http://www.dfes.gov.uk/dis/pdf/finaldisv5.pdf accessed 12 October 2004.

DfES (2004) *Departmental Report 2004*. London, DfES. Online. Available http://www.dfes.gov.uk/deptreport2004/ accessed 12 October 2004.

Dolton, P. and Vignoles, A. (1999) 'The impact of school quality on labour market success in the UK'. *University of Newcastle Discussion Paper*, 98–103.

Dolton, P. and Vignoles, A. (2000) 'The effects of school quality on pupil outcomes: an overview'. In H. Heijke (ed.) *Education, Training and Employment in the Knowledge-Based Economy*. Basingstoke: Macmillan.

Dolton, P., Vignoles, A. and Levačić, R. (2004) 'The economic impact of schooling resources'. In C. Sofer (ed.) *Human Capital over the Life Cycle: A European perspective*. Edward Elgar, chapter 3.

Dustmann, C., Rajah, N. and van Soest, A. (2003) 'Class size, education and wages'. *The Economic Journal*, 113 (February).

Feinstein, L. and Symons, J. (1999) 'Attainment in secondary school'. *Oxford Economic Papers*, 51, 300–21.

Finn, J.D. and Achilles, C. M. (1999) 'Tennessee's class size study: findings, implications, misconceptions'. *Educational Evaluation and Policy Analysis*, 21, 2, 97–109.

Fuller, B. and Clarke, P. (1994) 'Raising school effects while ignoring culture? Local conditions and the influence of classroom tools, rules and pedagogy'. *Review of Educational Research*, 64, 1, 119–57.

Glewwe, P. and Jacoby, H. (1994) 'Student achievement and schooling choice in low-income countries: evidence from Ghana'. *Journal of Human Resources*, XXIX, 3, 843–63.

Goldstein, H. (1995) *Multilevel Statistical Models*. London: Arnold.

Graddy, K. and Stevens, M. (2003) 'The impact of school inputs on student performance: an empirical study of private schools in the UK'. SSRN electronic paper collection. Online. Available http://econpapers.hhs.se/paper/cprceprdp/3776.htm accessed 14 September 2004.

Gujarati, D.N. (1995) *Basic Econometrics*. New York: McGraw Hill.

Gunasekara, J. and Levačić, R. (2004) 'Evaluating the effectiveness of Swedish International Development Authority (SIDA) funded primary education projects in Sri Lanka'. Paper presented at International Congress for School Effectiveness and School Improvement, Rotterdam.

Hallinger, P. and Heck, R. (1998) 'Exploring the principal's contribution to school effectiveness: 1980–1995'. *School Effectiveness and School Improvement*, 9, 2, 157–91.

Hanushek, E.A. (1979) 'Conceptual and empirical issues in the estimation of education production functions'. *Journal of Human Resources*, 14, 3, 351–88.

— (1986) 'The economics of schooling: production and efficiency in public schools'. *Journal of Economic Literature*, 24, 3, 1141–77.

— (1997) 'Assessing the effects of school resources on student performance: an update'. *Education Evaluation and Policy Analysis*, 19, 2, 141–64.

— (1998) 'Conclusions and controversies about the effectiveness of school resources'. *Economic Policy Review*, 4, 1, 11–27.

Hanushek, E., Rivkin, S.G. and Taylor, L.L. (1996) 'Aggregation and the estimated effects of school success'. *The Review of Economics and Statistics*, 78, 611–27.

Harbison, R., W., and Hanushek, E. (1992) *Educational Performance of the Poor: Lessons from rural Northeast Brazil*. Oxford: Oxford University Press.

Heckman, J. J. (2000) 'Causal parameters and policy analysis in economics: a twentieth century retrospective'. *The Quarterly Journal of Economics*, February, 45–97.

Hedges, L.V., Laine, R.D. and Greenwald, R. (1994) 'Does money matter? A meta-analysis of studies of the effects of differential school inputs on student outcomes'. *Educational Researcher*, 23, 5–14.

Hough, J. (1981) *A Study of School Costs*. Slough: National Foundation for Educational Research.

— (1991) 'Input-output analysis in education in the UK: a review essay'. *Economics of Education Review*, 10, 1, 73–81.

Iacovou, M. (2002) 'Class size in the early years: is smaller really better?' *Education Economics*, 10, 3, 261–90.

Kennedy, P. (1998) *A Guide to Econometrics*. Oxford: Blackwell.

Krueger, A. (2003) 'Economic considerations and class size'. *Economic Journal*, 113.

Krueger, A. and Whitmore, D.M. (2001) 'The effect of attending small classes in the early grades of college-test taking and middle school test results: evidence from Project STAR'. *The Economic Journal*, 111, January, 1–28.

Leibenstein, H. (1966) 'Allocative efficiency v. x-inefficiency'. *American Economic Review*, LVI, 3, 392–415.

Leithwood, K. and Jantzi, D. (2000) 'The effects of transformational leadership on organizational conditions and student engagement with school'. *Journal of Educational Administration*, 38, 2, 112–23.

Levačić, R. and Feinstein, L. (2001) *Approaches to evaluation of the relationship between school resources and student outcomes*. London: DfES.

Levačić, R. and Jenkins, A. (2004 forthcoming) 'Evaluating the effectiveness of specialist schools in England'. Centre for Economics of Education Discussion Paper.

Levačić, R., Jenkins, A. and Vignoles, A., Steele, F. and Allen, R. (2004) 'Estimating the relationships between school resources and pupil attainment at Key Stage 3'. Mimeo. Institute of Education, University of London.

Levačić, R. and Vignoles, A. (2002) 'Researching the links between school resources and student outcomes in the UK: a review of issues and evidence'. *Education Economics*, 10, 3, 312–31.

Levin, H.M. (1997) 'Raising school productivity: an x-efficiency approach'. *Economics of Education Review*, 16, 3, 303–11.

Little, D. (1998) *Microfoundations, Method, and Causation: On the philosophy of the social sciences*. New Brunswick, NJ: Transaction Publishers.

Machin, S. and McNally, S. (2004) 'The literacy hour'. London: Centre for Economic Performance, LSE.

Machin, S., McNally, S. and Meghir, S. (2003) 'Excellence in Cities: evaluation of an education policy in disadvantaged areas'. Unpublished working paper. London: Centre for Economics of Education, LSE.

Marsh, A. J. (2002) *Resourcing Additional and Special Educational Needs in England: 10 Years On (1992–2002)*. Slough: National Foundation for Educational Research.

Mayston, D. (2002) *Tackling the Endogeneity Problem when Estimating the Relationship between School Spending and Student Outcomes, Research Report 328*. London: DfEE.

McKim, V.R. and Turner, S.P. (1997) *Causality in Crisis? Statistical methods and the search for causal knowledge in the social sciences*. Notre Dame, Indiana: University of Notre Dame Press.

Meghir, C. and Palme, M. (2001) 'The effect of a social experiment in education'. Centre for Economics of Education Discussion Paper.

Muijs, D. and Reynolds, D. (2002) 'The effectiveness of the use of learning support assistants in improving the mathematics achievement of low achieving pupils in primary schools'. ICSEI, Copenhagen 2002.

Mulford, B., Silins, H. and Leithwood, K. (2004) *Leadership for Organisational Learning and Student Outcomes*. Lisse: Swets and Zeitlinger.

Nye, B., Hedges, L. and Konstantopoulos, K. (2002) 'Do low-achieving students benefit more from small classes? Evidence from the Tennessee class size experiment'. *Educational Evaluation and Policy Analysis*, 24, 3, 2001–218.

PriceWaterhouseCoopers (2000) *Building Performance: An empirical assessment of the relationship between schools capital investment and pupil performance: Research Report RR242*. London: DfEE.

PriceWaterhouseCoopers and Institute of Education (2003) *Researching the Relationship between Resourcing and Pupil Attainment: Final report to DfES*. London: DFES internal report.

Pritchett, L. and Filmer, D. (1999) 'What education production functions *really* show: a positive theory of education expenditures'. *Economics of Education Review*, 18, 223–39.

Rasbash, J. *et al.* (2000) *A User's Guide to MLwiN*. London: Institute of Education, University of London.

Ritter, G. and Boruch, R. (1999) 'The political and institutional origins of a randomized controlled trial on elementary school class size: Tennessee's Project STAR'. *Educational Evaluation and Policy Analysis*, 21, 2, 111–26.

Salmon, W. (1998) *Causality and Explanation*. Oxford: Oxford University Press.

Scheerens, J. (1997) 'Conceptual models and theory-embedded principles on effective schooling'. *School Effectiveness and School Improvement*, 8, 3, 269–310.

— (1999) 'Concepts and theories of school effectiveness'. In A.J. Visscher (ed.) *Managing Schools Towards High Performance*. Lisse: Swets and Zeitlinger, 37–70.

Schumacker, R.E. and Lomax, R.G. (1996) *A Beginner's Guide to Structural Equation Modeling*. Mahwah, NJ: Lawrence Erlbaum Associates.

Sobel, M. E. (1998) 'Causal inference in statistical models of the process of socio-economic achievement: a case-study'. *Sociological Methods and Research*, 27, 2, 318.

Tashakkori, A. and Teddlie, C. (2003) *Handbook of mixed methods in social and behavioral research*. Thousand Oaks, CA: Sage Publications.

Teddlie, C. and Reynolds, D. (eds) (1999) *The International Handbook of School Effectiveness Research*. London: RoutledgeFalmer.

Todd, P. and Wolpin, K. (2003) 'On the specification and estimation of the production function for cognitive achievement'. *The Economic Journal*, 113, February.

Vignoles, A.,Levačić, R., Walker, J., Machin, S. and Reynolds, D. (2000) *The Relationship between Resource Allocation and Pupil Attainment: A review. Research Report RR228*. London: DfEE.

Worthington, A.C. (2001) 'An empirical survey of frontier efficiency measurement techniques in education'. *Education Economics*, 9, 3, 245–68.